TITMICE

First published in Great Britain in 1998 by
Colin Baxter Photography Ltd
Grantown-on-Spey
Moray, PH26 3NA
Scotland

Text © Keith Graham 1998
All rights reserved

A CIP Catalogue record for this book is available from the British Library

ISBN 1-900455-53-6

Photographs © 1998:

Front Cover © Mark Hamblin
Back Cover © Chris Gomersall
Page 1 © Laurie Campbell (NHPA)
Page 4 © Neil McIntyre
Page 6 © Michel Strobino (Oxford Scientific Films)
Page 9 © Melvin Grey (NHPA)
Page 10 © Paal Hermansen (NHPA)
Page 13 © Neil McIntyre
Page 14 © Janos Jurka
Page 19 © Christian Meyer
Page 20 © Stephen Dalton (NHPA)
Page 23 © Laurie Campbell

Page 26 © Laurie Campbell
Page 28 © Neil McIntyre
Page 31 © Roger Tidman (NHPA)
Page 32 © Christian Meyer
Page 35 © David Whitaker
Page 37 © Laurie Campbell
Page 38 © Laurie Campbell
Page 41 © Laurie Campbell (NHPA)
Page 43 © Geoff Du Feu (Planet Earth Pictures)
Page 44 © Neil McIntyre
Page 45 © Laurie Campbell

Printed in Hong Kong

TITMICE

Keith Graham

Colin Baxter Photography, Grantown-on-Spey, Scotland

Contents

Titmice

The remarkable growth in bird-watching as a hobby in Britain, is perhaps best brought into focus by the countless folk who are now able to indulge in armchair bird-watching. Burgeoning populations of small birds which now live and breed in the parks and gardens of the suburbs of our towns and cities, have opened the eyes and ears of suburban dwellers to a whole new world. Above all perhaps, it is the small, colourful and highly active members of the titmouse family which are at the forefront of this avian revolution and which most often become the main attractions.

Statistics gathered by the MORI poll organisation indicate a rapid growth in the number of adults in Britain who feed wild birds in their gardens which, according to the polls, had risen from 50% in 1994 to 67% in 1996. Such figures in themselves are a measure of the growing level of interest in garden birds. Add to that the millions of pounds spent annually by residents of the UK on the purchase of bird food and it is clear that garden bird-watching is one of the nation's most popular hobbies. A considerable proportion of that expenditure is devoted to the purchase of peanuts, to which members of the titmouse family, most notably the agile blue tits, great tits and coal tits, are particularly attracted.

There are 53 different species of titmouse in the world which are classified into three general groups, Parinae, Aegithalinae and Reminzinae. Britain boasts seven true members of the race, of which the most familiar are the blue tit, great tit and coal tit, all of which come readily to gardens in both town and country. Where they are common, most often in rural areas, marsh and willow tits are also sometimes tempted by such artificial food sources. Long-tailed tits are increasingly to be seen exploring garden vegetation but the other true tit is much more limited and specialised in its range. The crested tit is to be found in Scotland where it prefers the remaining remnants of the Caledonian Pine Forest, once a dominant landscape feature of the Scottish Highlands.

The great tit, another familiar garden visitor and the largest of Britain's titmice.

There is an eighth bird which has been generally listed with the titmice but which is, strictly speaking, not a tit at all but a member of a largely Asian group of birds known as Parrot-bills. The bearded tit, or bearded reedling, restricted in its range to the East Midlands and south-east of England, being especially prevalent in East Anglia, is now recognised as being of a different family altogether, albeit that it displays the agility and attractiveness typical of true tits. Unlike the true tits, which are all by nature woodland dwellers, the bearded tit is a resident of marsh reed beds.

Despite their enthusiasm for nuts, seeds and fat, tits are primarily insect eaters. Moreover, the two most popular and numerous members of the tit clan, the blue tit and great tit, are avid consumers of caterpillars, especially when they are rearing their young families, and are thus recognised by gardeners as extremely effective pest controllers.

The natural nesting habitats of these two tits are holes and crevices in trees or rocks, but they also take exceptionally well to nest boxes, further underlining their willingness to establish home territories in parks and gardens. They can also be seen exploring garden trees and shrubs for their harvests of spiders and other small insects.

All titmice are attractive to look at but the demeanour, again especially of the colourful blue tits and great tits, is probably what catches the eye and what most people enjoy watching. Both not only exhibit considerable agility, dexterously clinging on to nut containers or halved coconuts, but also display a high degree of intelligence in their quest for food. Hence, great tits especially have been the focus of scientific research work over the years. A remarkable number of experiments have been devised to test and measure this apparent intelligence and the tits seem to always come out with high grade passes. Indeed there is some suggestion that great tits, in particular, can count.

Perhaps the great tit has been chosen as the principal subject of this kind of research because it is naturally bold and aggressive, takes readily to nest boxes and is very willing to live cheek-by-jowl with mankind, thus making observation relatively straightforward and activity easy to record. However, it is perhaps the pugnacious,

An adult long-tailed tit with a caterpillar, the most important source of food for all titmice chicks.

A willow tit frolicking in the snow. Difficult to distinguish from the marsh tit, they are only rarely seen in urban areas and although sometimes visiting rural bird-tables, they are more often seen in deciduous woodland.

action-packed and fearlessly 'cheeky' attitude displayed especially by great tits and blue tits, which appeals to so many people.

But why titmouse? The word itself has ancient origins. Although it might be imagined that the small nature of all members of the tit family forges a natural association with the notoriously small mouse, the origins of this part of the name are instead to be found in the Old English language in which the word *mase* – evolving into mose and later, mouse – meant small bird. The English language has evolved from many sources and the tit part of the word can be traced to the Icelandic word *tittr* which also means small. If these two words which both mean 'small', naturally seem to fit these small and active birds, doubtless the use of the word 'mouse' to describe them owes much to their small size and active nature.

Most tits are by nature woodland birds but the migration of large numbers to suburbia owes much to the new artificial sources of food, especially during the winter months. In many respects we have, in our gardens, recreated a new kind of woodland which in turn attracts the invertebrates upon which the tits naturally feed.

There has been a gradual movement northwards by populations of the most numerous of the titmice, blue tits and great tits, so that now they breed throughout mainland Britain and Ireland and recently have begun to colonise the islands north and west of mainland Scotland, possibly encouraged by a succession of milder winters. The coal tit, too, has joined in this general expansion. Although not as numerous, the coal tit is particularly fond of coniferous woodland, and the increased afforestation of recent years will have been a further encouragement for it to colonise new areas. The coal tit is also increasingly numerous in suburban gardens, albeit in smaller numbers compared with the other two more familiar tits.

Similarly, the long-tailed tit is known to breed throughout mainland Britain but its preference for low-level deciduous woodland has perhaps discouraged it from colonising many of the Scottish islands. However, recent surveys (1997) indicate that long-tailed tits are prospering and that their British populations may well have reached record levels. While these attractive members of the tit family seem hesitant to exploit bird-table offerings, they are now seen with much greater regularity in and around suburban parks and gardens.

There has also been a limited recent expansion northwards by the marsh tit, although its extremely close similarity to the willow tit may have led to some confusion between the two, thus clouding the issue. These two, almost identical, birds (they were only recognised as separate species at the beginning of this century) are most common in southern parts of the British Isles, although there seems to have been some colonisation by the marsh tit northwards during the second half of the twentieth century.

Nevertheless, records from the early part of the twentieth century indicate that the willow tit was once more common in parts of Scotland than is now the case, breeding as far north as Angus on the east coast, from where it is now largely absent. These two titmice are much more prevalent in England and Wales, although both are absent from Ireland. Neither has followed the lead of their more familiar cousins by migrating into built-up areas, although both are regular visitors to rural bird-tables.

Like the willow tit, the crested tit excavates its own nest. The range of the crested tit, essentially a forest bird, is more restricted than any other tit, the main concentrations occurring in the remnant pine forests of Moray, Deeside and Strathspey in Scotland. It may be assumed that before the widespread destruction of the Caledonian pine forest of Highland Scotland, crested tits were much more widely distributed. Nesting preference is focused upon dead tree stumps and it is the female which excavates the nest itself. However, crested tits also take well to nest boxes. Nesting sites seem most often to be sited relatively low, typically less than 13 ft (4 m) above the ground.

These then are the members of the titmouse family familiar to residents of Britain. Each, apart from the almost identical willow and marsh tits, is distinctly different in appearance, colour and marking and each exudes its own particular charm. Above all, it is those universal characteristics of pugnacity, agility, boldness and liveliness which make them surely the most popular of our small native birds.

In Britain, the crested tit is found in pine forests in the north-east of Scotland.

The Great Tit

The largest of our native tits, the great tit is also perhaps the most pugnacious of them all. Observation of great tits feeding at a bird-table or on a basket of nuts soon reveals an intolerance not only of other great tits but often of every other avian visitor to that particular 'honey-pot'. The aggression with which they are imbued is quickly manifested by the opening of their wings, a menacing hissing, the lowering and pointing of the head and often a full frontal attack upon all comers. Indeed, there are times when it seems some great tits spend more time repelling 'all boarders' than they do actually feeding.

Known sometimes as the 'ox-eye' because of its large, white facial patches or cheeks, it is a handsome creature. The bright yellow chest, split by a black line – bolder and longer in the male than the female – is offset by the glossy black cap which merges with an equally black chin, chest and collar. Only at the nape of the neck is the pattern broken. Here, the green plumage of the bird's back invades the back of the black cap, as if a barber has used his cutters to create a curious 'wedge'. The wings are a blueish-grey which, when open, reveal a curved white wing bar with some of the flight feathers bearing a faint yellow edging. The tail too is grey apart from the two outer feathers which are white, a unique variation not found in any other tit.

The great tit with which we are so familiar (*Parus major major*) is present throughout Europe and northern Asia, right across the Palearctic as far east as China. There are other sub-species to be found in the Far East which are less boldly coloured with only a hint of yellow on the breast (*Parus major minor*) and two others in the Indian sub-continent and as far south as Indonesia (*Parus major cinereus*) and in Central Asia (*Parus major bokharensis*) which are in essence black, grey and white in colour, lacking any hint of yellow.

The well-known versatility of the great tit is further underlined by the wide variety of vocalisations it has at its command. One noted ornithologist has suggested that many otherwise unidentified bird sounds in woodland probably emanate from great tits. Most

A pair of great tits, female to the left. The broad black breast band is longer and bolder in the male.

familiarly, the strident 'tea-cher, tea-cher, tea-cher' is its commonest vocal hallmark.

Research has shown that there may be as many as forty variations upon a theme, an indication perhaps that male great tits which have enlarged their repertoire may indeed become more desirable as potential mates. It may be presumed that if this is so, further variations on that theme are yet to be developed.

In spite of their renowned agility, great tits are more likely than any of the titmice to spend time foraging for food on the ground. Their superior size may make them fractionally less agile than, for instance, the much smaller blue tits. This is also reflected in the fact that great tits are more likely also to forage for food on bird-tables themselves.

Deciduous woodland is the most favoured habitat but they are becoming increasingly familiar in coniferous woodland and also adapt well to hedgerows in otherwise un-wooded farmland.

Their diet, too, shows interesting diversity. In the autumn, they feed extensively on beech-mast and thus many of them are inclined to desert upland woods in favour of beech woods at that time of the year. However, the British population is extremely sedentary and has been estimated to number well over ten million and to be essentially stable. By contrast, great tits in continental Europe are much more vagrant in their lifestyle, sometimes, when populations reach high levels, they migrate to explore new territories.

From time to time continentally based birds erupt and arrive in parts of Britain both in spring and autumn, notably in south-east England. The more northerly birds of Scandinavia also, of necessity, migrate southwards in the winter.

Like many small birds, the lifestyle of great tits varies from season to season. There is, for example, the phenomenon of flocking, often with other tits during the winter months, in which the advantage of many pairs of eyes enhances the collective search for food sources. It is well known that flocks of small birds are less vulnerable to predation.

But, as even the most casual observer of birds would quickly recognise, the approach of spring stimulates greater independence and a desire to establish individual territory and attract a suitable mate. The establishment and defence of great tit territories certainly bring out that well-known characteristic of belligerence, particularly in the male birds.

The timing of this growing spirit of independence varies considerably from year to year according to prevailing weather conditions. It is quite often the case that benign and mild conditions, even in January, can stimulate this spirit of enterprise and alert the biological changes which occur in the reproductive organs.

Whether sooner or later, the mood certainly changes as spring advances. It is now that the variety of song comes into play. As is the case in most birds, it is the female which makes most of the vital choices. She selects the most eligible mate (the one that impresses her most with his physical appearance, vigour and song). And it is she who makes the choice of nest site, the male having previously selected a number of potential sites for her inspection.

At this time the male strikes a number of postures such as stretching himself vertically, head and beak pointing upwards with the full splendour of his bold black chest band exposed for inspection. In the most splendid males, this black band broadens between the legs and runs the entire length of the male's body to the underparts of the tail, and is a major factor in the female's ultimate selection of her mate.

Of course, several males may compete not only for territorial possession but for mates as well and it is then that full-scale aggression can be observed with rival cocks pointing aggressively at each other, wings lowered and the beak, the main weapon, pointing directly at the rival, or as a male flies assertively towards a rival in an undulating display.

The driving force for the female is of course, to find the best possible father for her offspring, the natural law employed by all birds, the end product of which is a healthier, stronger, future generation.

Once the choice is made, the serious business of procreation follows but not before the female has assessed the quality of the chosen territory. A nest, even if it contains masses of material, can be constructed in a relatively short time but the female may take her time, spending several days roosting at the nest site, often in it, in order to assess the food potential in its immediate vicinity. She may also be assessing the male's capability in terms of his defence qualities against possible predators.

If the potential seems poor, she may well desert, 'divorcing' a mate perceived to be inadequate and leaving her new home, perhaps to find another mate in possession of a more food-yielding territory. But if all seems well, the process of nest building will begin in earnest. The female is the nest builder, packing vast quantities of moss into the bottom of the nest and finally adding hair or fur, forming a cup for the eventual nursery for her young.

Timing of course, is of the essence. Close observation is made of the activities of the neighbourhood moths especially, the caterpillars of which will, in due course, become the most important food source for the chicks. If their cycle is started early, then so too must the cycle of the tits' breeding activities, otherwise their chances of success will be severely affected.

In our observations of birds, we are generally unaware of the importance of their alertness to what is going on around them. Cuckoos keep a close watch over the behaviour of the birds they will select as surrogate parents for their offspring. For them too, timing is vital. In cuckoos that observation is obvious and visible, much less so perhaps in smaller birds such as the tits, but clearly it is an on-going preoccupation.

The availability of food sources will also play a part in the ultimate clutch size. More food will encourage the laying of more eggs, less will restrict clutch size. Winter moth caterpillars are an important food source for great tits residing in oak woodland. Their life cycle is clearly concomitant with the timing of the emergence of the food plants upon which the caterpillars themselves feed. It is therefore not just a simple matter of temperature or date. The whole process is inextricably linked to the progress of a complex series of other life forms.

And of course, other factors come into play. Great tits which live in oak woodlands tend to produce more eggs than, for instance, hedgerow-based birds, a reflection

Great tit feeding young. A large brood of chicks can consume 7-8000 caterpillars over three weeks.

Among the most belligerent of Britain's native birds, the great tit, here seen
mounting a full frontal attack on a possible rival, is a doughty defender
of territory. But it is the female which makes the choice of
a suitable mate when it comes to pairing.

presumably of a greater abundance of food. It follows that in a poor spring, when food is judged to be at a premium, clutch size is accordingly reduced.

When at last the process begins, the eggs, between 8 and 12 of them, white with a scattering of brownish-red spots, are duly laid and incubation begins by the female alone. If she leaves the nest, the eggs are covered by nesting material to ensure that the correct temperature is maintained. In all, the brooding lasts for about 14 days, the female fed by the male. Once the eggs hatch, it is all hands to the pumps and over the ensuing three weeks, the two parent birds have to work extremely hard gathering more and more food as their brood grows.

It has been calculated that during the rearing period of three weeks, a single pair of great tits may have to find 7-8000 caterpillars in order to sustain a large brood of youngsters, which are hatched naked and blind. From late April through the month of May, the timing of this exercise depending upon all the other factors already mentioned, the parent birds literally do have to work every hour of daylight that is available to sustain their chicks which eventually leave the nest at about three weeks of age.

Over the course of a year food choice and availability naturally vary widely according to the seasons. It follows that insects and insect larvae dominate during the summer months, while there is a greater dependency upon food of a vegetable nature when insect food is at a premium in the winter months.

Studies of great tit behaviour in relation to food foraging have intrigued scientists and revealed not only the physical dexterity and coordination of great tits but also their persistence and mental ability when it comes to solving puzzles posed by researchers. Scientific experiments which have required great tits to pass a number of tests (for example, removing obstacles or tapping with their beaks in order to open containers) whilst in themselves proving their considerable learning ability and ingenuity, are nevertheless academic and do not relate directly to life as it is lived by these birds in the wild.

Many observers of great tits in gardens will know that they are well able to exploit nuts suspended on a cord by simply pulling up the cord and holding it with their feet, loop after loop, until each nut is reached. Similarly, when tits are exploiting a wild food source such as a nut or caterpillar, they can sometimes be seen holding the object with their feet and attacking it with vigorous pecks of their strong beak. Sometimes there is a variation on a theme when the bird jams a nut into a suitable crevice so that it can attack it in situ.

The most remarkable observation, however, was of a great tit using a pine needle to extract larvae from holes, in other words as a tool with which to tease out its victims. Great tits are also very alive to the hoarding habits of other birds such as coal and marsh tits, often making careful observation of where such caches are being hidden and then simply helping themselves.

The greatest threats to great tits are posed by weasels which are agile climbers and slender and sinuous enough to penetrate nesting holes in trees, where they may devour either eggs or chicks. Once a clutch of chicks has fledged, sparrowhawks take a heavy toll, especially of young, inexperienced birds, which have not yet fully developed their flying skills.

The loss of a clutch or brood may lead to a second clutch being laid, often within a very short space of time. In Britain second clutches – other than when a first is lost – are relatively rare, an indication that as things stand, survival numbers are high enough to sustain current populations.

The Blue Tit

Even more numerous than great tits are the smaller blue tits, widely distributed throughout Britain and Ireland. They are also found throughout Europe and in western Asia but their range is much more restricted than that of the great tit. However, there are few places in these islands where this active and attractive little bird is not now found, save for the farthest flung islands and the most mountainous terrain of the Scottish Highlands.

The blue tit is perhaps even more popular than the great tit, celebrated for its

Alert and agile, the blue tit rejoices in many local names, most appropriately, 'Bluebonnet'.

remarkable agility and its ability to cling to almost any surface, if necessary upside down, and notably to containers of peanuts or fat, or to halved coconut shells.

Blue tits were also at the forefront of avian opportunism when they discovered that they could supplement their diet by pecking through the foil caps of milk bottles and consume the fat-rich cream on top of the milk, a clear example of learned behaviour and an indication that these little tits are also imbued with a high degree of intelligence. Great tits soon followed the lead given to them by blue tits.

The antics of blue tits feeding upon the food placed in the garden of my childhood home, became the object of my own first conscious close encounters with birds. Equally, I am sure that the same could be said by countless other folk. Like great tits, blue tits have been the subject of considerable scientific research. They too pass tests with flying colours and are able, for instance, to open matchboxes in order to obtain food, or remove a series of pegs which in turn also release food to them.

Several curious traits in blue tit behaviour have been noted. For example, a blue tit accidentally finding itself inside a house, may begin to pull small strips of wallpaper from the walls. It may be concluded that such activity mirrors the habit of these inquisitive little birds when they strip tree bark back in order to reach insects and larvae beneath. Their attacks upon putty securing window glass may have a similar association with the habit of searching through moss, soft bark and in crevices for insect and larval food.

Courtship procedure is similar to that of the great tit and almost as assertive, with territories guarded with equal belligerence. On benign January days in woodland and gardens the high-pitched trills of blue tits signify the approach of the breeding season but nesting sites are often not chosen until February or March, again dependent upon conditions.

Blue tits take readily to nest boxes as alternatives to the more natural tree holes and crevices. To attract either blue tits or great tits to nest in your garden, it is important to have suitable nest boxes in place at least by mid February and preferably earlier. It is preferable to site such boxes on the north side of a tree or wall so they are not exposed to the full strength of the summer sun.

Displays and confrontations not unlike those performed by competing male great tits are also the hallmark of cock blue tits. However, here again it is the female which makes the choices of mate and indeed of ultimate nesting site. The ways in which she makes these choices are very similar to the methods employed by a hen great tit: she will have regard to the food-yielding potential of the environs of a suitable nesting site and will probably 'test' it and her mate's potential during nest building.

However there is one difference in behaviour between the two species in that the cock blue tit is an enthusiastic helper of his mate during nest building, clearly a part of the bonding process. This is accentuated by the proffering of food by the male, by wing shivering displays and by posturing and the raising of his little blue head crest.

Once established, mating and the laying of eggs begin in April or May. Up to 15 eggs may be laid, which are very similar to those of the great tit, white with blotches of red, and take a mere 14 days to hatch. Brooding is the prerogative of the female.

The average clutch size for blue tits in Britain is said to be between 11 and 12. However, the mortality rate is estimated to be around 70%. Thus, it is easy to see why blue tits in particular go for large families, a necessity if populations are to be sustained. As with the great tits, the real work comes during the following three weeks as the youngsters, also hatched naked and blind, place ever-increasing demands upon the parent birds, a period during which thousands of caterpillars and aphids are caught by the parents.

Caterpillars are the main source of food for the youngsters, which fledge at about 20 days. If ever there was a time to confirm that blue tits are 'all action' birds, then that time is certainly during this crucial rearing period. It is not a good idea to provide nuts when the adults are feeding their young. While instinct will tell them that caterpillars and insects are in any case a far more protein-rich food for rapidly growing youngsters, should there be a dearth of such food, they may resort to trying to use nuts, which are extremely indigestible for young birds, with fatal consequences.

Like the great tit, one brood is usually sufficient, although second broods are by no means unknown and are often the result of the loss of the first clutch. The success of

Ablutions! All birds have to take great care of their plumage and this blue tit is no exception. Feather care is the order of the day and bathing is an important part of that process. Sometimes birds take dust baths as they try to keep their plumage clean and free from parasites.

second broods will naturally be limited by the availability of food. However, it would seem that the overall population of blue tits is comfortably sustained by one reproductive cycle per year.

The emergence from the nest of the youngsters, at about three weeks, is manifested in the comical rows of them usually perched close to the nest, noisily greeting each visit of their parents who continue to ply them with food. At this time they are especially vulnerable; the weasel and sparrowhawk are the main natural predators upon blue tits, although in suburbia, domestic cats undoubtedly take a heavy toll. Grey squirrels also include the eggs and chicks of blue tits on their diet sheet and can gnaw their way into nest boxes. The size of the entrance hole to a blue tit nesting box is also crucial. If it is too big, other birds can gain access, typically in suburban gardens, sparrows. Equally, if there are woodpeckers in the vicinity, they too may try to enlarge the hole and take the box over. The ideal diameter for the hole in a blue tit box is 1.1 in (2.8 cm). If you have woodpeckers, a metal plate round the hole offers some protection but for effective defence against all predators, nest boxes of concrete and other hard materials can now be purchased.

Once the breeding season has come to an end and the parent birds have moulted, community life begins anew. Blue tits often join marauding bands of other tits, together with a few tree-creepers and, in southern Britain, nuthatches, adopting the flock mentality for the common good both in terms of finding food and as a deterrent to predators. Towards the end of summer, their lifestyle has changed and more activity becomes apparent in gardens. However, unless it is an uncommonly cold late summer and early autumn, they will spend more time foraging for insects than seeking artificial food such as peanuts.

Hard winters can be difficult for all small birds. One clear disadvantage of being small is that the bird has a large body area relative to overall size and thus on particularly cold winter nights, can lose energy at a rapid rate. It is therefore vital, should you start to feed the birds in your garden, that the supply should be constant. The local population of birds will come to rely on the food you provide and any break in that

continuity, even for a day or two, especially in adverse conditions, can cost many birds their lives.

Blue tits, especially, provide rich entertainment with their acrobatic quest for food, their 'perkiness' and of course their attractive appearance. The cobalt blue skull cap sits at a jaunty angle above a white forehead. The eyes are given a slightly oriental appearance by the dark, navy blue eye-stripes and the cheeks are bold and white. The green plumage of the back invades in a less obtrusive way at the nape of the neck, compared with the great tit; the back is green and the chest yellow with a central band of blue, variable in size and seemingly not markedly different between male and female. The wings too are blue with a curved white band. The blue tit is therefore handsome, action packed, agile and a real entertainer, surely one of the most popular of all our garden birds.

The Coal Tit

Deriving its name from the dense black cap with which it is adorned, the coal tit is also a frequenter of parks and gardens but generally in a much more covert way. It is the smallest of our native tits and is particularly prevalent in coniferous woodland. The expansion of forestry throughout Britain has therefore ensured that numbers of coal tits have risen in recent decades. However, before the destruction of the natural woodlands, especially in Scotland, it may, long ago, have been even more commonplace.

Coal tits are widespread throughout Europe and right across Asia into China. They are, like the other familiar tits, extremely sedentary, seldom moving far from their home range except when there are severe food shortages.

The coal tit is a rather more delicate feeder than its more bullish cousins, picking rather than hammering at nuts as might be expected of the possessor of a much finer bill, which is the perfect tool for extracting from nooks and crannies the tiny spiders, aphids, grubs and other larvae which are its preferred food choices. In autumn and winter, seeds of plants such as thistles are also consumed.

Although frequently seen in gardens, conifer forest is the more rural habitat for coal tits.

Some have described the coal tit as being drab compared with the more exotic and colourful-looking great tits and blue tits. Although it lacks the rich coloration of its compatriots and boasts no yellow at all (except in newly fledged youngsters and in the Irish race of coal tits), it is nevertheless a most attractive little bird, in some respects even sharper and quicker in its movements than other tits.

Its plumage is a mixture of olive, buff and grey except for the underparts which are pale, almost white, merging to an orange-tinted buff to the rear. A coal black head, white cheek patches and the curious wedge of white at the nape of the neck, are the hallmarks of this particularly active little bird. The black chin extends into its chest – more so than, for instance, in the case of the great tit – and its head seems disproportionately large. The wings have a double white bar which helps identification in flight.

The courtship of the coal tit is manifested in displays of wing fluttering, with the tail spread and little parading displays by the male in which he droops his wings and holds his tail erect. The same basic ground rules apply. Territory is established by the male in the latter weeks of winter. In proclaiming its patch, the coal tit's voice, thinner and higher pitched than the great tit, nevertheless reflects a similar kind of rhythm, if somewhat less assertive: 'teechuu, teechuu, teechuu', often followed by a brief, flourishing trill.

The nest, the site of which is chosen by the female, is usually quite low, often in a rotten tree-stump but sometimes even at ground level where on occasions an old mouse hole is taken over. Holes in banks or walls are used and coal tits do take readily to nesting boxes.

In general, coal tits are not quite as quick off the mark compared with great tits and blue tits but the range of food is marginally greater, a reflection of its finer beak which is clearly not quite as strong when it comes to attacking nuts.

The female contributes most of the nest building effort, collecting and arranging considerable quantities of animal hair, although the cock birds do help, again presumably as part of the bonding process.

Between 7 and 12 eggs, white speckled with red, are laid in late April or early May, incubated by the female alone for about 14 days and, as with its other tit compatriots,

The coal tit seems to have a disproportionately large head and is easily recognised by the light coloured wedge at the nape of the neck.

A huddle of young long-tailed tits. They are among the most sociable of birds, living out most of their lives in close communities in which parental duties are often undertaken by non-breeding members of the community.

the fledging period is relatively long for such a small bird, about 16 days. Young tits probably take slightly longer to fledge than the chicks of other small birds because of the greater security provided by nesting holes as compared with the built nests of, say, finches, which are more exposed. The greater variety of food offered to the chicks probably means that timing is not quite as crucial as is the case with great tits and blue tits. Coal tit hens are notoriously brave in the defence of their eggs and young, sitting tight and hissing menacingly at any intruder.

Extremely agile, coal tits can often be seen clinging perilously to pine needles as they search every little recess for the tiny insects in which they delight. Coal tits are also assiduous hoarders of food, concealing surpluses beneath fallen pine needles, in clumps of moss and behind tree bark, a confirmation of their sedentary lifestyle.

The Long-Tailed Tit

In many people's eyes the most enchanting of all the tits, both in appearance and lifestyle, long-tailed tits are primarily inhabitants of lowland deciduous woodland. They are increasingly appearing in suburban parks and gardens but seldom exploit artificial food sources, their main prey comprising insects and spiders and only occasionally, seeds and buds. As its name suggests, this little bird has an inordinately long tail, much longer than its body which as a consequence gives the bird's body the appearance of a tiny, delicate, black, white and pink ball.

This is essentially a community-minded bird, at all times of the year, even during the breeding season when long-tailed tits nest in little colonies. Indeed, they take community life to the extreme, non-breeding members of the community even helping to care for the youngsters of other members of the group.

The long-tailed tit is also widespread right across Europe and Asia and the northern race shows slight variations of plumage, namely a pure white head. The birds with which we are familiar in Britain are delightfully marked with black facial flashes above the eyes and a white crown, light, almost white underparts which merge to pink on the lower body, dark wings and pink back surmounted by a dark central patch. The tail which accounts for 3 in (7.6 cm) of the bird's total length of about 5.5 in (14 cm), is black, delicately framed in white.

The passage of a little flock of long-tailed tits is often marked by their characteristic and constant vocal communication, a high pitched but soft 'si-si-si'. They seem always to work in concert, travelling through woodland or along hedgerows together and filtering through the branches as they search out the tiny insects and spiders which are their staple diet.

The most remarkable facet of their breeding season is the construction of the nest. It is a domed, intricate structure made of mosses, lichens and cobwebs and lined with feathers, usually built in the fork of a tree or hedgerow. The most amazing aspect of the nest of a long-tailed tit is surely the lining which is made up of feathers. Nests that have been examined reveal a content of no fewer than 2000 feathers, in itself a tribute to the dedication of the pair of birds which, working in concert, have collected every last item for this remarkable piece of bird architecture. Where nests have been found close to towns or cities, and especially where air pollution negates the presence of lichen, scraps of paper and polystyrene are sometimes used as substitutes.

Courtship in such a community-orientated bird is unsurprisingly less assertive and seems mainly to involve a chase through the trees or a slower, almost hovering flight by the male to demonstrate to the female his prowess.

The eggs are usually laid in April, between 8 and 12, white and lightly marked with red blotches. Occupation of the nest requires the sitting bird, most often the female, to fold her long tail back over her back. As added security, she generally positions herself in such a way that the tail covers the little entrance hole near the top of the nest.

For 16 days she incubates and, once hatched, the youngsters grow so rapidly that they are able to leave the nest at 14 days. It is then that other adults which have either failed to hatch eggs, or not bred at all, can be seen caring for youngsters, even feeding

The long-tailed tit's intricate, dome-shaped nest may contain as many as 2000 tiny feathers.

them, while the true parents are away on food foraging missions. At first the youngsters do not bear the same facial markings as adult birds, being much browner, the tail not yet fully grown.

In their constant and restless quest for food in trees and hedgerows, long-tailed tits exhibit the same degree of agility as the other titmice, frequently to be seen clinging to the slenderest twigs, upside down, sometimes hanging on with one foot while holding a morsel of food in the other and nibbling at it. For security purposes, as they pass from tree to tree, they do not travel in one mass but in twos and threes, creating the impression that they are never still. Their community lifestyle continues in the winter when on cold nights a group of them will huddle together for warmth.

Delightful birds in every way, wonderful nest builders and extremely communally minded, long-tailed tits – if rather less likely to be seen about bird-tables – are nevertheless, among the most watchable and attractive of our native small birds.

The Marsh Tit & Willow Tit

Confusion reigns when it comes to discriminating between marsh and willow tits. Their markings are almost identical, both are much more commonly found in southern parts of Britain and both, by and large, avoid urban areas. Indeed it was only in 1900 that these two birds were given individual identities. Both are similar in size to the blue tit, both are basically brown birds above and pale beneath and both possess a distinguished and very black cap, more sooty in the case of the willow tit, glossy in the marsh tit. The willow tit also has distinguishing pale patches on its wings and a notably larger head, almost out of proportion to the rest of its body, and a rounder body than the marsh tit.

They differ only slightly in their choice of habitat, the marsh tit preferring drier broad-leaved woodland, willow tits, conifers and danker deciduous woods. The marsh tit is content to use an existing hole in which to build its nest whereas the willow tit is busier, excavating its own nest, a flask-shaped hole, up to 1 ft (0.3 m) in depth, usually in

The glossy black cap of this marsh tit distinguishes it from the very similar willow tit.

a rotten tree-stump, evidence of which is seen in the litter of excavated wood chippings beneath the nest site. Occasionally willow tits will occupy nest boxes but only if the box in question has been partly filled with softish material it can excavate. Both pack their nests with a mixture of grass, bark, wood chips and hair.

The marsh tit is found in many parts of Europe and in complete isolation in China too, whereas the willow tit can be found right across Europe and Asia. Neither are present in Ireland; in Scotland the main concentrations of marsh tits are in the south-east whereas willow tits are mainly to be found in the south-west.

The willow tit is also somewhat more musical, in the spring producing a quite pleasing and fluent, high-pitched warble, while the marsh tit is confined to a repetitive two-note ditty of little musical quality. Both, at other times of the year, issue scolding little notes, delivered sometimes singly, sometimes in bursts.

Their food preferences are very similar, with insects the most important constituent part of the summer diet. Marsh tits are a little more willing to feed at bird-tables while willow tits are often to be seen feeding in low cover, regularly taking the seeds of weeds such as nettle. Neither seems overly attracted by the notion of joining together in flocks and are perhaps the least community minded of all the titmice. Courtship is like that of the coal tit in that the males parade around the females, tails held erect, plumage fluffed out and wings drooped. Both are relatively covert in lifestyle compared with the bolder and more familiar titmice

Late April and early May are the favoured egg-laying months. Clutches are generally smaller in number than those of other tits, six to eight, but incubation, conducted by the females, is about the same, 14 days, and the youngsters leave the nest at about 16 days old.

The Crested Tit

This is the least commonplace of our native tits. Primarily restricted to the remnants of the Caledonian pine forest which once swathed so much of Highland Scotland, the

The crested tit is Britain's most specialised and rarest member of the titmouse clan.

crested tit was once much more widely distributed. However the destruction of these natural forests over a long period of time, which was probably at its height in the seventeenth and eighteenth centuries, has undoubtedly reduced the range of this highly attractive little bird.

There have been encouraging signs of limited expansions west and south from the areas around the Moray Firth, Deeside and Strathspey where its main breeding areas lie, and the current enthusiasm to regenerate the remaining pine forests will undoubtedly help further expansion in the future.

The crested tit is quite well distributed elsewhere in Europe, and is fairly common in the forests of Scandinavia, its range stretching well into Russia, but not far into Asia. In Britain, it has never been recorded breeding outside Scotland.

Only the coal tit, among members of the British titmouse family, is smaller than the crested tit. Even then there is little in it… about a quarter of an inch. The most obvious physical feature is the black and white head crest which is raised prominently during courtship. The crest is of black feathers flecked with white and, like many of its titmice cousins, it also boasts light cheek patches, boldly outlined by a black semicircle from the eye. The neck is white, further outlined by a black collar which extends at the front to give the bird a black chin. Its upper body is of a greyish-brown, its underparts characteristically light.

Like many of the other tits, the crested tit is extremely agile as it hunts for food and its fine little beak is the ideal tool for extracting the tiny insects and insect larvae that are its staple diet. Caterpillars, aphids and spiders are important during the summer months but at other times of the year they sometimes revert to pine seeds and the fruits of, for instance, juniper.

Like the willow tit, the crested tit often excavates its own nest, usually in the trunk of a rotten pine stump and relatively close to the ground. Sometimes, however, they will exploit natural holes which require little or no excavation work.

Vocally, the crested tit is rather less assertive than many of the other tits, the most often heard, 'tsi-tsi-tsi', somewhat gently delivered. Yet in behaviour, the typical alertness of mind and quickness of movement exhibited by other tits are equally inherent.

I recall an interesting encounter while trying to photograph ospreys at Loch Garten from one of the RSPB's forward hides. At one juncture, a crested tit began to display typical curiosity and for a few moments actually perched on the end of my long lens. Not surprisingly, I failed to capture it on film!

During courtship the male chases the female in an excited manner, sometimes rising high above the tree tops, trilling all the while to advertise his wares. As pairing begins, the male will ceremonially feed the female and it may be presumed that the more offerings he is able to make, the more chance he has of being 'the chosen one'. He also indulges in wing fluttering displays.

Crested tits generally produce only five or six eggs which are similar to other titmouse eggs, white with little reddish spots. The nest is extensively lined by the female although the male assists with the gathering of deer hair, wool and feathers. She takes entire responsibility for incubation which lasts about 14 days, the youngsters flying about 18 days after hatching.

The crested tit is the least commonplace of our native tits.

Quite often a crested tit can be observed feeding in much the same way as a treecreeper, working its way up and down the bark of a tree, using its minuscule but strong sharp claws to cling on. However, they seem reluctant to become community-minded in the winter months, seldom if ever joining other mixed flocks of small birds.

The Bearded Tit

The bearded tit is, strictly speaking, not a tit at all. However it exhibits many tit-like traits, such as agility, especially among the reed beds which are its preferred habitat. It is also a very attractively plumaged bird, tawny of back, grey of head and possessor of a fine, flowing 'moustache' of black which descends from its eyes to the neck on either side of the face. It also has a long tail and strongly marked wings.

In the days of the nineteenth century and the era of caged birds, it was much sought after. It is hard to imagine that such a bird could take kindly to captivity for it is by preference a bird of covert lifestyle, spending much of its life among the reeds seeking out insects and seeds. On quiet days, you may see them dancing just above the reeds in their quest for food on fast whirring wings, uttering their little staccato 'pinging' notes.

Recent expansions of their populations from East Anglia into Essex and Kent have been mirrored elsewhere as for instance in Holland where they have colonised reclaimed, reedy land. They range across Central Europe and into Asia but other populations exist in isolation, in the Far East. One success story is worthy of mention in that they have been so productive at the Minsmere Reserve of the RSPB in Suffolk, that there are often autumn emigrations from that reserve to other surrounding areas.

In the courtship display the male raises the feathers on his crown, puffs out his fine moustache and spreads the feathers of his tail. In response the female also spreads her tail and dances, before both birds rise slowly in a bonding flight. The nest, built by both birds, is situated in reed beds surprisingly close to the water's surface, constructed of sedges and dead reeds and lined with grass to which the male adds reed flowers as an extra decoration. Five to seven eggs are laid, creamy with distinct brown markings. Incubation is shared between male and female and lasts a mere 13 days. The youngsters are extremely precocious, able to leave the nest at 10 to 12 days. They have particularly brightly coloured inner mouths, an added stimulus to the feeding parents.

Unlike the true tits, bearded tits are production line breeders, often beginning the process quite early in April, and continuing throughout the summer, sometimes rearing as many as three or even four broods in a season.

Now officially known as the 'bearded reedling' the bearded tit is not, strictly speaking, a fully paid-up member of the titmouse clan. It is exclusively a bird of reed beds and most commonly seen in East Anglia.

The willingness of blue tits, great tits and coal tits especially, to flock to gardens to exploit the food put out for them, has been at the root of the remarkable growth in bird-watching as a hobby. The antics of these birds, as they cling perilously to the nut containers, now such a familiar part of most gardens, give everyone, young and old, a perfect opportunity to watch at close quarters some of our most attractive birds.

Titmice Facts

GREAT TIT

Family: Paridae
Latin name: *Parus major*
Length: 5.5 in (13–14 cm)
Description: Glossy black head and neck, white cheeks, black band on yellow chest (more prominent in male), green back, white edging on outer tail feathers.
Habitat: A preference for broad-leaved woodland but also present in coniferous woodland, hedgerows, parks and gardens.
Nesting: Tree holes or crevices in rocks, walls etc. Takes readily to nest boxes. Packs considerable quantities of moss, hair and down into nesting cavity.
Eggs: 8–12, white, boldly spotted with reddish brown. Incubated by female, 13–14 days. Nestlings fed by both parents, fly after 19–20 days.
Food: Mostly insects, including caterpillars (especially when rearing young), aphids, buds, fruit, seeds, nuts and beechmast.
Some local names: Black Cap, Black-headed Tomtit, Ox-eye, Saw Sharpener, Saw Finch, Charbonniere, Joe Bent, Heckymal, Pick Cheese, Pridden Pal, Tomtit.

BLUE TIT

Family: Paridae
Latin name: *Parus caeruleus*
Length: 4.5 in (12–13 cm)
Description: Wings, tail and crown of head blue, white cheeks, green back, yellow underparts.
Habitat: Woodland of all types, with marginal preference for deciduous woods. A popular garden bird.
Nesting: Tree hole or crevice in wall. Takes well to nest boxes. Nest building by both with considerable quantity of grass, moss, hair and wool packed into nesting cavity.
Eggs: 8–15, white with reddish brown spots. Incubated by female for 14 days. Nestlings fed by both parents, fly after 19–20 days.
Food: Aphids, spiders, caterpillars (especially to young) and other insects. Some fruit, seed and nuts. Avid consumers of peanuts and fat (eg; suet) in gardens.
Some local names: Allecampagne, Bluebonnet, Bluecap, Blue Ox-eye, Blue Tom Tit, Blue Whaup, Bottle Tit, Hickwall, Jerrybo, Stonechat, Tom Tit, Blue Spick, Nun, Titmal.

COAL TIT

Family: Paridae
Latin name: *Parus ater*
Length: 4.25 in (10–11 cms)
Description: Glossy black head with white flash at nape. Olive grey back, black bib, pale underparts merging with buff.
Habitat: Coniferous woodland but also found in deciduous woodland and parks and gardens.
Nesting: Dead tree stumps, holes in banks or walls, deserted mouse burrows. Cavity extensively lined with hair, moss and feathers, built by both sexes.
Eggs: 6–10, white with reddish brown speckles. Incubated by female for 14 days. Young fed by both parents. Fly after about 16 days.
Food: Insects: flies and larvae, grubs, spiders and caterpillars. Seeds of nettles and thistles, some nuts.

Some local names: Blackcap, Black Ox-eye, Cole Tit, Caley Tit, Coalhead, Cole Mouse, Coal Hooden, Coaly Hood, Tomtit.

LONG-TAILED TIT

Family: Aegithalidae
Latin name: *Aegithalus caudatus*
Length: 5.5 in (13–14cm)
Description: Long black and white tail, pink, black and white plumage, black and white striped head.
Habitat: Deciduous woodland and hedgerows. Now more common in gardens.
Nesting: Builds intricate domed structure, often wedged into tree fork, made of moss, lichen, cobwebs and lined with feathers, with access hole near top. Built by both sexes.
Eggs: 8–12, white with reddish speckles. Incubated by female for 16 days. Youngsters fed by both parents. Fly after 14 days.
Food: Insects and spiders with some buds and seeds.
Some local names: Barrel Tit, Bottle Tit, Bottle Tom, Caper Longtail, Ekimol, Feather Poke, French Magpie, Long-tailed Pie, Long Tom, Mufflin, Nimble Tailor, Oven bird, Oven Builder, Tree Huck-Muck, Ragamuffin, Juffit, Fuffit, Hedge Mumruffin, Jack in a Bottle, Long-tailed Chittering.

MARSH AND WILLOW TIT

Family: Paridae
Latin name: Marsh Tit, *Parus palustris* / Willow Tit, *Parus montanus*
Length: 4.5 in (11–12 cm) (both)
Descriptions: Marsh Tit has black, glossy cap and grey, brown upper parts and dull, whitish buff underparts. Willow Tit has sootier, duller black cap, a conspicuously larger head and a rounder body. It is most easily distinguished by the pale patches on its wings, absent in the Marsh Tit.
Habitats: Both are woodland birds but the Marsh Tit much prefers broad-leaved woodland whereas the Willow Tit is more often found in coniferous woods and danker deciduous woodland.
Nesting: Marsh Tit uses tree-holes or crevices, packing nest with hair, down and moss. Willow Tit also uses tree holes but often excavates rotten tree stumps, creating a considerable cavity, similarly lined by both parents.
Eggs: 6–8 eggs, white with red-brown speckles, incubated by females only for 14 days. Youngsters fed by both parents. Fly after about 16 days.
Food: Wide variety of insects plus some seeds and fruits. Willow Tit more inclined to feed on seeds of nettles and thistles.
Some local names: Marsh Titmouse, Willow Biter, Black Cap (both), Saw Whetter, Black Headed Tit, Coalhead, Smaller Ox-eye.

CRESTED TIT

Family: Paridae
Latin name: *Parus cristatus*
Length: 4.5 in (10–11 cm)
Description: Black crest edged with white, black facial semi circle, greyish-brown back.
Habitat: Exclusively pine or spruce woodland but most commonly in old pine forests of north-east Scotland.
Nesting: Excavates hole in rotting tree stump usually within 4 ft (1.2 m) of ground. Sometimes uses existing holes and takes readily to nest boxes.

Eggs: 5–6, white with reddish brown spots. Incubated by female only for 14 days. Fed by both parents. Fly after about 18 days.

Food: Insects, aphids, caterpillars and occasionally pine seeds and juniper berries.

Some local names: None known

BEARDED TIT

(Now known as the Bearded Reedling)

Family: Muscicapidae

Latin name: *Punurus biarmicus*

Length: 6.5 in (16–18 cm) (including tail)

Description: Tawny back, tail and wings (wings also contain black and white feathers). Female also has tawny head but male head grey, decorated with bold black moustache. Pale underparts.

Habitat: Reed beds in marshland or at waterside locations.

Nesting: Built from sedges, reeds and grasses low (just above water) in reed beds. Male lines nest with reed flowers.

Eggs: 5-7, cream with distinct brown markings. Incubated by female for about 13 days. Fed by both parents. Fly after 9–12 days.

Food: Insects, insect larvae and other invertebrates. Occasionally reed seeds, notably in winter.

Some local names: Reed Bunting, Bearded Pinnock, Reedling, Beardmanica, Reed Pheasant, Least Butcher Bird.

Recommended Reading

AA & RSPB, *The Complete Book of British Birds*, AA & RSPB, 1988.

Gosler, Andrew, *The Great Tit*, Hamlyn Limited, 1993.

Greenoak, Fransesca, *All the Birds of the Air*, Andre Deutsch, London, 1979.

Oddie, Bill, *Bill Oddie's Little Black Bird Book*, Eyre Methuen, London, 1980.

Perrins, C.M., *British Tits*, Collins, London, 1979.

Sharrock, J. T. R., *The Atlas of Breeding Birds in Britain and Ireland*, British Trust for Ornithology, 1977.

Thom, Valerie, *Birds in Scotland*, T. & A. D. Poyser Ltd, Staffordshire, for the Scottish Ornithologists' Club, 1986.

Biographical Note

It was probably the antics of members of the titmice in the garden of his childhood, which first sparked an interest in wildlife for Keith Graham. That interest quickly burgeoned and became a waking passion, so much that a good deal of his life has been devoted to watching, recording and understanding the sometimes complex relationships between birds and human beings. Keith has been a long-time resident of Perthshire, where Highland meets Lowland, a landscape he knows particularly well after pioneering the Countryside Ranger Service in that area of the country. Indeed it is that diverse landscape which remains the inspiration to him. His weekly columns in the *Stirling Observer* and *Perthshire Advertiser*, which he has been writing now for some 23 years, in their own way reflect his constant search for a greater understanding of the birds and animals he observes and studies. This is the fourth book he has written in the Colin Baxter WorldLife Library series, his previous books in this series are *Foxes*, *Hares* and *Owls*.